Making T-shirt Yarn

Creating your own T-shirt yarn ensures that you have control over all the parts of your project from start to finish, and can be a fun part of the process. Whether purchasing T-shirts from your local craft store or picking them up at a thrift store, look for larger sizes so you will have more T-shirt yarn when finished. I always purchase at least an XL. Be sure to check the stretch of the T-shirt prior to purchasing it, as not all T-shirts are suitable. To do this, place your hands on each side of the T-shirt just above the bottom hemline, then gently pull both sides of the T-shirt horizontally, stretching the fabric. As the fabric is stretched, it should begin to roll up and down from the stretched area. When strips are cut and pulled, they will roll into a tube. Inexpensive T-shirts made of 100% cotton and cotton blends work well.

There are two methods to cutting your T-shirt apart. Refer to the diagrams for a detailed illustration of both methods.

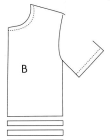

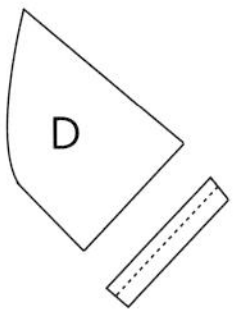

Separate strips.
Fold the T-shirt in half and place it onto a cutting mat (A). Using a ruler and a rotary cutter, cut the shirt into strips 1" (25mm) wide (B). Remove the sleeves and finish cutting the T-shirt top and sleeves as shown (C, D).

Continuous strip.
Remove the hemline. Start cutting into the bottom of the T-shirt on one side at an angle until you reach a 1" (25mm) depth on the far side. Continue cutting around the circumference of the T-shirt in one continuous strip until you reach the bottom of the sleeves (E). Remove the sleeves and finish cutting the T-shirt top and sleeves as shown (C, D).

this book I used a combination of purchased yarn and yarn I created. Purchasing a skein of yarn allows you to move directly to the dyeing process and ensures uniform yarn width and no weak spots in the yarn where scissors may have gone awry. Pre-purchased yarn is a good choice if you want to make a lot of projects in a short of amount of time—which may be the case during the holiday season. I recommend the brand Nooodles by Sullivans. It comes as a 100-gram skein and is comprised of 95% cotton and 5% spandex. The yarn dyes beautifully.

Spiral Size Chart

Each spiral used in this book is sized by its diameter or length when completed. To achieve each size spiral, use the appropriate length strip of T-shirt yarn as indicated by the table. Add extra inches to the drop spiral length as needed to create the drop. This chart is handy, but don't measure things obsessively—a little variety is welcome! Test a few spirals first, using the chart as a suggestion for lengths of yarn to be used. The finished size of the spirals you achieve depends greatly on how tightly they are wound. Adjust the lengths of yarn used accordingly.

		Spiral Size						
		½" (13mm)	¾" (19mm)	1" (25mm)	1¼" (32mm)	1½" (38mm)	1¾" (44mm)	2" (51mm)	3" (76mm)
Yarn Lengths	**Spiral**	3" (76mm)	4½" (114mm)	6" (152mm)	7½" (191mm)	9" (229mm)	10 ½" (267mm)	12" (305mm)	18" (457mm)
	Drop Spiral	3" (76mm)	4½" (114mm)	6" (152mm)	7½" (191mm)	9" (229mm)	10 ½" (267mm)	12" (305mm)	18" (457mm)
	Beaded Spiral	3½" (89mm)	5¼" (133mm)	7" (178mm)	8¾" (222mm)	10 ½" (267mm)	12¼" (311mm)	14" (356mm)	21" (533mm)
	S Spiral	9" (229mm)	11¼" (285mm)	13½" (343mm)	15¾" (399mm)	18" (457mm)	27" (687mm)		
	Teardrop	1½"(38mm)	2¼" (57mm)	3" (76mm)	3¾" (95mm)	4½" (114mm)	5¼" (133mm)	6" (152mm)	9" (229mm)

Custom Dyeing T-shirt Yarn

Dyeing your own yarn is a little bit messy but a lot of fun. The instructions are the same for dying purchased yarn or yarn you created yourself by cutting up T-shirts. Collect all your supplies and read all instructions before beginning. You'll be surprised at what kinds of cool color combinations result from the hand-dyeing process. Every batch is different.

SUPPLIES

- T-shirt yarn
- Dye
- Salt
- Water: boiling, hot, and cold
- Sink or basin
- Microwave
- Clear glass measuring cup
- Plastic wrap
- Scissors
- Teaspoon
- Squirt bottles
- Newsprint
- Gloves

Prep

Prepare your workspace.
Prepare your workspace by covering it with newsprint and then plastic wrap. Locating your workspace near a water source as well as an electrical outlet is ideal.

Bundle and wet yarn strips.
Lay about ten 48" (1220mm) T-shirt yarn strips, folded in half, on a flat surface. Cut two 6" (152mm) strips from the sleeve of the T-shirt (or the yarn skein); tie them around the 48" (1220mm) strips a few inches up from each end. (Note: tying the yarn together helps prevent tangling during the rinsing process.) Then, soak the yarn bundle completely, wring it out, and lay it on top of the plastic wrap on the prepared workspace. If using purchased yarn, form a bundle in a similar manner using approximately sixteen yards of yarn.

Dyeing

Mix the dyes. Shake all dye bottles before measuring the dye. Wearing rubber gloves, measure and mix 1 oz. dye with 1 oz. hot water (140°F) and 1 teaspoon salt. Pour the mixture into a squirt bottle, twist the bottle top on tightly, place your gloved finger over the opening, and shake vigorously. Then remove your finger, letting air into the bottle slowly to avoid spilling.

Dye with first color. Starting with the lightest color, squirt dye mix onto the yarn bundle, concentrating the color in a 2" (51mm) area and allowing the dye to flow outwards. Insert the bottle tip into the folds of the yarn and squeeze, again allowing the dye to flow towards the sides of the bundle. Repeat in multiple spots moving down the length of the yarn bundle. Leave plenty of space for additional colors.

Dye with second color.
Choose the second lightest color and dye more areas according to the directions in step 4.

Dye with other colors.
Dye more areas according to the directions in step 4 until all desired colors have been used. Then, turn the yarn bundle over and continue dying on the other side until the entire bundle is colored. Blot excess dye using a paper towel.

Wrap and microwave.
Lay the dyed bundle on a fresh piece of plastic wrap and fold the wrap around the bundle. Add additional plastic wrap until the bundle is completely covered on all sides and both ends. Place the bundle in a microwave and set the timer for two minutes on high.

Rinse and wash.
Carefully open the plastic wrap and rinse the bundle with cold water. Repeat until the water runs clear. Add a mild detergent to a sink or basin full of hot water, place the yarn in the water, and agitate using your hand or a stirring stick. Rinse the yarn thoroughly again in clean water. Dry the bundle in a dryer on a hot setting or set it aside to dry. Once the bundle is completely dry, untie it.

Tips & Techniques for Dyeing

Dyeing is a fun process but it can also be tricky to get things exactly right. Check out these tips before beginning, and you'll be sure to end up with great colors and little or no mess.

- The very best fabrics to dye are natural fabrics such as cotton, linen, and silk. You can also have success with synthetics such as rayon and nylon. Stay away from 100% polyester, acrylic, spandex, and metallic, as well as fabric listed as dry clean or cold water wash only. Fabric blends such as 50% cotton and 50% polyester will work, but be aware that the colors will not be as intense as they are with 100% cotton. Generally, the higher the percentage of natural fibers in a material, the brighter and clearer the colors will be within your project.

- When mixing custom colors, follow color charts, such as the charts located at www.ritdye.com/colorit_color_formula_guide. Checking the color guide prior to starting your project will provide inspiration as well as the necessary mixing formula.

- Mix only the amount of dye you will need for your project, because mixed dye cannot be stored. Use plastic or metal containers to mix the dye, and clean the containers immediately after use with hot water and detergent. The dye might stain plastic containers, so designate a few containers specifically for use with dye.

- To achieve bright, bold colors, always use water at 140°F/60°C when mixing dye. Having a kettle nearby to heat the water is extremely handy.

- When dying the bundle, leave white space between colors and allow time for the dye to flow. You can always go back and add more dye. If you have done your homework and your colors work together, the overlap will form a third, very desirable color.

- Colors in the yarn will look darker when wet and prior to washing.

- Use paper towels to blot excess dye from around the yarn bundle prior to wrapping it in plastic wrap. Gloves and an apron or old shirt are necessities when dyeing. And don't wear your favorite pants or white shoes, either!

- Take the time to thoroughly wrap the dyed yarn bundle in plastic wrap before microwaving. Adding an additional layer of plastic wrap just might save your microwave. Always place the wrapped bundle on the glass tray in your microwave. If dye leaks, clean the glass tray immediately with detergent.

Techniques

By learning a few basic techniques, you can create endless combinations of embellishments to design whatever accessories you like. With just five shapes and a few tying and finishing techniques, you will be able to make everything in this book and more. Practice on undyed scraps of T-shirt yarn and feel free to mess up—once you get the hang of it, manipulating the yarn will be like second nature.

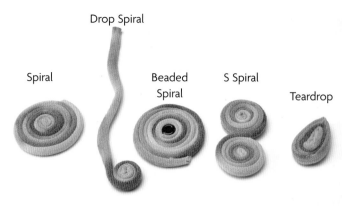

These are the five pieces that will be the basic embellishments for your jewelry and accessories. From left: spiral, drop spiral, beaded spiral, S spiral, and teardrop.

Basic Shapes

Five basic shapes are used throughout the projects in this book, and with a little practice you'll be making them faster than they can dry! The five shapes are the spiral, drop spiral, beaded spiral, S spiral, and teardrop. Each project calls for spirals of specific types and sizes; for example, you might need a 1" (25mm) spiral and a 2" (51mm) S spiral to make a project.

A 1" (25mm) spiral will use a 6" (152mm) long piece of T-shirt yarn, a 2" (51mm) spiral will use a 12" (305mm) long piece of yarn, etc. Use the chart on page 3 as a reference to make sure you have the right length of yarn to work with when making each type of spiral.

SPIRAL

Apply a drop of glue to one end of the rolled side of a T-shirt yarn strip. Fold the end into the glue. Roll the strip into itself, adding glue as you go and wrapping to form a spiral of the desired size. Trim away the excess yarn and glue the loose end to the spiral.

BEADED SPIRAL

Apply glue to the outside edge of a plastic pony bead and wrap a T-shirt yarn strip around the bead firmly. Continue wrapping and adding glue as you go to form a spiral of the desired size. Trim away the excess yarn and glue the loose end to the spiral.

DROP SPIRAL

Create a spiral according to the directions under Spiral, but instead of gluing the short trimmed end to the spiral, leave a longer tail of the desired length to form the drop.

S SPIRAL

Start with an 18" (457mm) strip of T-shirt yarn. First, mark the midpoint at 9" (229mm). Apply a drop of glue to one end of the rolled side and fold the end into the glue. Roll the strip into itself, adding glue as you go and wrapping to form a spiral all the way to the midpoint. Next, add a drop of glue to the non-rolled side on the opposite tip of the yarn, fold the end into the glue, and wrap to form a spiral, rolling in towards the spiral you already made. When the two spirals meet, add an additional drop of glue.

TEARDROP

Apply a drop of glue to one end of the rolled side of the T-shirt yarn strip. Fold the strip over ½" (13mm) and press into the glue. Fold the strip around itself, adding glue as you go and pinching the top of the spiral to form a teardrop shape of the desired size. Trim away the excess yarn.

Finishing with Closures

The projects in this book each use one or more of the following techniques to create the closure for the accessory.

BEAD PULL-THROUGH

This closure uses two yarn strands (the loose ends of the necklace or bracelet), a pony bead, and a simple overhand knot. By threading the two yarn strands through the bead, you create a super easy and super adjustable closure. This closure is used in the Braided Anklet (page 14), the Sophisticated Spiral Trio Necklace (page 16), and the Tonal Teardrop Necklace (page 18).

Feed two T-shirt yarn strips (each end of the necklace or accessory) through a single pony bead from opposite ends to form the closure. Tie overhand knots at the desired length and trim.

DOUBLE KNOTTED ADJUSTABLE CLOSURE

This closure is used in projects with four loose yarn ends. By knotting the strands to one another using two semi-loose knots, you create a closure whose knots will slide closer or farther apart without changing the look of the bracelet. That way, one accessory can be adjusted to fit and grow with its wearer. This closure is used in the Friendship Bracelet (page 12), the Spiral Bracelet (page 14), and the Sophisticated Spiral Trio Bracelet (page 17).

Lay the bracelet or other accessory on a flat surface with the end strips in a loose circle with both ends crossing over each other. Select one end set of strips, and tie the ends of these strips (using an overhand knot) to the other set of strips about halfway down their length. Do the same for the other side: take the long strips and tie them midway down on the opposite strips. Adjust the knots to achieve the desired fit. Tie overhand knots to the loose ends of each of the strips, slide these small knots down next to the adjustable sliding knots, and trim. To adjust the size of the bracelet, gently pull on the strip ends to move the larger adjustable knots.

Overhand Knot and Double Knot

The simple overhand knot is the only knot necessary for many of the projects in this book. Create the overhand knot according to the photo and pull tight. A double knot is very similar to the overhand knot, but uses two strips or ends of yarn instead of one, and is just like starting to tie your shoes: cross the two ends, fold one end up and under the other, tighten, and repeat once more.

LOOP CLOSURE

The Loop Closure technique makes a simple necklace piece into an additional decoration. Any necklace that features a "pendant" made of spirals can use this closure. By using this closure, you have two necklace strands instead of one. The Loop Closure technique is used in the Statement Necklace (page 15).

Cut a 15" (381mm) strip of T-shirt yarn, fold back each of the ends to form a loop, and glue the loops closed. Glue the strip to the back of the necklace, being sure to glue it all along the length so that it is secure and hidden. This may take some creative maneuvering if your necklace is a funky shape! Once this looped piece is secure, insert another long piece of yarn through the loops straight across: through one loop from the outside of the necklace to the inside, then through the second loop from the inside to the outside. Once the strip is through, tug the piece that is between the loops until it is the desired length of the necklace. Tie the two loose ends together using an overhand knot.

WRAP AND KNOT

This technique is used in projects that are made with many strands of T-shirt yarn (more than 4). It is more of a technique to create the body of a bracelet than it is a technique to make a closure, but the loose strands that are left at the end are used for a Bead Pull-Through closure. In this technique, yarn is bundled and tied together, glued securely in place, and trimmed to create solid ends. The Wrap and Knot technique is used to make the Braided Anklet (page 14).

1

Lay out strips. Holding the desired number of base T-shirt yarn strips together, form a 3" (76mm) loop using a separate strip that is at least 12" (305mm) long. Place the loop on top of and running parallel to the base yarn strips. The top of the loop should be even with the top of the base strips.

2
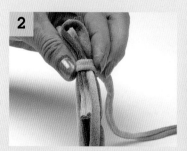

Bundle and wrap. Holding the top end of the loop firmly against the base strips, wrap the long end of the looped strip around the base strips three times.

3

Start the knot. Insert the long end upwards through the loop.

4
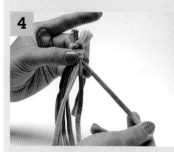

Finish the knot. Pull down the opposite end (the short strip hanging down from the loop) to close the loop, trapping the long end of the strip under the wrapped strips.

5
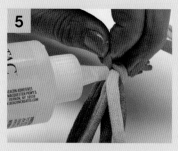

Trim the short strip. Trim the end of the short strip and add a drop of glue, pushing the trimmed end under the wrap.

6

Trim and glue. Hold the end of the long wrapped strip (hanging out from the top) out of the way and trim all of the base strips next to the wrap. Add glue to the trimmed ends to prevent movement and fraying. Now, the single strand will become the strand used for the Bead Pull-Through closure when you repeat these steps for the other end of the Wrap and Knot bundle.

Hair Accessories

Jazz up your hairdo with one of these two super-useful and super-fun projects. Clip your hair back with a sweet barrette or go get active after pulling your hair into a ponytail with a hair elastic.

Barrettes

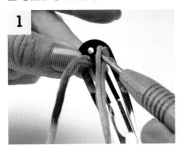

Thread the yarn. Insert the ends of a 10" (254mm) piece of T-shirt yarn through the holes in the base of the barrette.

Attach the spiral. Create one 1½" (38mm) beaded spiral for each barrette. Using the needle tool or a toothpick, insert the yarn ends through the beaded spiral one at a time.

Knot and finish. Pull the two ends taut, bringing the barrette up against the bottom of the beaded spiral. Tie a bow. Tie overhand knots to the ends of the strips and trim the excess.

SUPPLIES

- ◇ Hand-dyed T-shirt yarn
- ◇ Hair barrette blanks
- ◇ Hair elastics
- ◇ Pony beads
- ◇ Needle tool or heavy-duty toothpick
- ◇ Scissors

Hair Elastics

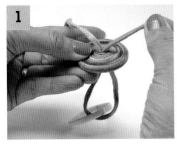

Loop the spiral. Create one 2" (51mm) beaded spiral and two 1" (25mm) beaded spirals for each hair elastic. Insert one end of a 10" (254mm) piece of T-shirt yarn through the hole in the 2" (51mm) beaded spiral. Loop the yarn around the hair elastic and insert the second end of the yarn through the bead.

Attach the spiral. Pull the two yarn ends taut, bringing the elastic up against the bottom of the beaded spiral. Tie a double knot.

Add the bobbles. Insert each of the yarn ends through the centers of one of the 1" (25mm) beaded spirals and tie overhand knots, leaving about 1½" (38mm) of space. Trim the excess.

Needle Tools

A needle tool (pictured in the Barrettes photos) is an inexpensive item you can buy in a craft store that makes threading materials through holes easier. To use a needle tool, just push the T-shirt strip through the center of the bead or other hole. Then, when you push a second strip through, hold the first strip taut against the side of the bead to allow the second strip to pass through easily.

Headbands

Start off with a project that can be as simple or as detailed as you like: a fun, comfy headband with three great embellishment options that can be made to match any outfit.

SUPPLIES

- ◇ Hand-dyed T-shirt yarn
- ◇ Plastic headbands
- ◇ Heavy-duty double-sided tape
- ◇ Fabric marker
- ◇ Scissors

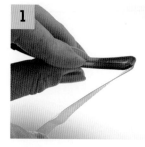

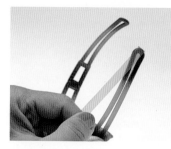

Start to tape. Apply a long strip of double-sided tape (with backing left on one side) to the inside edge of one end of the headband, approximately 1" (25mm) in. Wrap the tape around the bottom to the front edge.

Apply tape. Continue applying tape along the top of the headband, wrapping it back around the opposite end of the headband and trimming.

Start the yarn. Remove the backing from the tape and press one end of a T-shirt yarn strip, unrolled, into the tape.

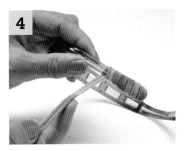

4

Wrap the yarn. Wrap the yarn up around the end of the headband, and continue wrapping it around the headband, ending either in the center of the headband or off to one side depending on the desired embellishment style. The seam will be covered with the embellishment.

5

Repeat. Repeat, wrapping the yarn around the headband from the opposite end until the two strips meet. Press the yarn into the tape to assure strong adhesion. Now you have your basic headband to embellish as desired.

Embellishment Options

Use one of these three embellishment options or think up your own! There is an embellishment for every personality. The Fun Fob is totally funky; the Spirals are sophisticated; and the Lots of Knots are somewhere in between.

Fun Fob

Cut eight 10" (254mm) strips of yarn and gather them at the center point. Wrap another 10" (254mm) strip around the crown of the headband and over the center of the strips, then tie a double knot to secure the eight strips to the headband. Tie overhand knots to the end of each strip, sliding the knot down to about 1" (25mm) above the headband and trimming the excess above the knot. Wrap another 10" (254mm) strip around the bottom of all of the strips, parallel to the headband, and tie a double knot. (This will boost the eight strips so that they do not lie flat against the headband.) Trim the ends of this double knot and add a drop of glue.

Spirals

Create one 1¾" (44mm) spiral, one 1½" (38mm) spiral, and one 2" (51mm) S spiral (1" [25mm]) per half of S). Glue the two spirals over the seam of the headband, placing their raw edges together. Glue the S spiral on top of the spirals.

Lots of Knots

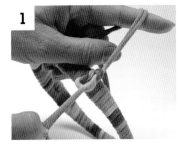

1

Knot on yarn strips. Cover the crown of the headband by tying multiple short yarn strips around it. Secure each strip with a double knot as shown.

2

Knot the ends. Then, tie overhand knots to the loose ends of each strip, sliding the knot down close to the headband and trimming the excess above the knot. If you like, make them in different lengths.

Friendship Bracelets

Matching friendship bracelets make great gifts, and you can make as many as you like for all your friends.

SUPPLIES

◇ Hand-dyed T-shirt yarn

◇ White plastic oval or rectangular sliders

◇ Alphabet stickers

◇ Pony beads

◇ Needle tool or heavy-duty toothpick

◇ Scissors

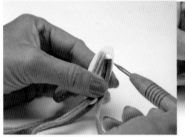 

Cut two 16" (406mm) T-shirt yarn strips and insert them through both openings of the slider, pulling the strips taut against the underside of the slider. Using the needle tool, slide one pony bead down each set of strips. Create a Double Knotted Adjustable Closure to finish the bracelet (see page 7).

Decorating with Stickers

Initials and acronyms such as BFF (best friends forever) work wonderfully when decorating small bracelet sliders and oval charms. When spelling out names, start from the  middle to ensure that spacing is even. And it's not necessary for all the letters to be perfectly aligned—tilt them a little in different directions for a more visually interesting piece.

Rings

In just five minutes you can create a standout accessory in one of two interesting varieties. Make many and give them as little gifts to friends and family—you don't need a reason or a holiday!

Swirled Cap Ring

Create one 1½" (38mm) spiral. Cover the top side of the ring base with glue and press the spiral on firmly.

Ring with Bow

Create one 2" (51mm) beaded spiral. Cut a 10" (254mm) T-shirt yarn strip and insert both ends through the beaded spiral, leaving a loop at the bottom. Try the ring on the wearer, adjusting the loop until it fits comfortably. Start tying a double knot, but finish with a bow. Tie overhand knots to each of the loose yarn strips and trim the excess. Add a touch of glue underneath the knot on top of the spiral to ensure that the knot doesn't loosen or pull through.

SUPPLIES

◇ Hand-dyed T-shirt yarn

◇ Ring blanks

◇ Fabric glue

◇ Pony bead

◇ Scissors

Flip-Flops

Not only are these flip-flops one-of-a-kind, but their straps are also cushioned with T-shirt yarn so they are completely comfortable. Select one of three great embellishment styles.

SUPPLIES

- ◇ Hand-dyed T-shirt yarn
- ◇ Flip-flops
- ◇ Heavy-duty double-sided tape
- ◇ Fabric glue
- ◇ Needle tool or heavy-duty toothpick
- ◇ Scissors

Embellishment Options

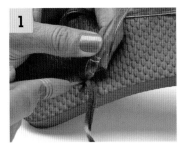

Tape and begin. Cut two 50" (1270mm) T-shirt yarn strips for each pair of flip-flops. Apply double-sided tape to the tops of the flip-flop straps. (At this point, peel off the backing just a little bit at the base of the flip-flop where the back strap is attached; this will make it easier to remove completely in the next step.) Starting at one side, add a drop of glue and insert the end of one yarn strip into the base of the flip-flop where the back strap is attached. Be sure to push it in deeply and securely.

Wrap the straps. Remove the rest of the backing from the tape and start wrapping the yarn strip around the flip-flop strap, pressing the yarn strip into the tape as you wrap. Continue wrapping until you reach the base of the flip-flop strap on the opposite side. Trim the strip, leaving enough to add a drop of glue and insert securely into the base of the strap, as you did in step 1.

Spirals

Create two 2" (51mm), four 1" (25mm), and four ¾" (19mm) spirals for each pair of flip-flops. Glue the spirals to the top of the wrapped flip-flops, starting with the largest spiral at the center, adding the medium spirals to either side, and then finishing with the smallest spirals.

Crazy Fob

Cut twenty-four 5" (127mm) strips. Wrap a 10" (254mm) strip around the center of the 5" (127mm) strips and tie the bundle to the front of the flip-flop strap, wrapping the tie strip around the strap twice and securing with a double knot. Trim the strips to the desired length.

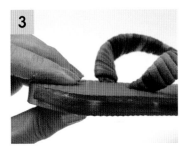

Finish. Use glue to add a single strip of yarn to the outer rim of the flip-flop. Alternatively, cover the entire rim using three rows of yarn. Start and finish the rows at the heel of the flip-flop.

Bow

Wrap some yarn around your hand three times, leaving some extra loose at the beginning and end. Remove the bundle of yarn from your hand. Form a bow by tying a 10" (254mm) strip around the center of the bundle. Trim all four loose ends to the desired length and glue the bow to the front of the flip-flop strap.

Classic Bracelet & Anklet

Two very different accessories can each be created in a few simple steps. You can make them to match and wear them together, or design each piece separately to go with special outfits.

SUPPLIES
- Hand-dyed T-shirt yarn
- Fabric glue
- Needle tool or heavy-duty toothpick
- Scissors

Spiral Bracelet

Assemble the spirals. Create two 1 ½" (38mm) and one 1 ¼" (32mm) beaded spiral. Lay the two spirals next to each other on a flat surface, leaving a small space between them. Center the beaded spiral on top of the two larger spirals and glue it in place. Do not block any of the bead openings.

Thread the yarn. Cut two 16" (406mm) yarn strips. Fold one strip in half and insert the fold upwards through the bead at the center of the beaded spiral.

Assemble the bracelet. Slide the second 16" (406mm) strip through the loop formed by the first strip and lay it across the surface of the small spiral. Insert each of its ends down through the beads of the two large spirals. Pull the top loop down taut against the small spiral.

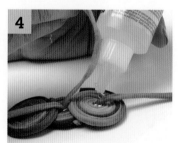

Finish the bracelet. Add glue to the hanging strips along the underside of the bracelet to hold them flat against the spirals. Create a Double Knotted Adjustable Closure to finish the piece (see page 7).

Braided Anklet

1 **Wrap and knot.** Cut six 20" (508mm) T-shirt yarn strips and lay them on a flat surface next to each other. Wrap and knot one end by following the Wrap and Knot instructions in the Techniques section on page 8.

2 **Braid.** Divide the six strips into three groups and braid to the desired length. Wrap and knot again when you reach the end.

Trim. Trim above the knots as per the Wrap and Knot instructions. This will leave a single yarn strip extending from either side of the braid. Add a drop of glue to the freshly trimmed ends to secure them. Create a Bead Pull-Through closure to complete the project (see page 7).

Statement Necklace

Are you ready for a necklace that stands out? Despite its complex appearance, this necklace is surprisingly simple to make. Just layer and glue the spirals and you'll have a big, bold accessory to show off.

SUPPLIES
- ◇ Hand-dyed T-shirt yarn
- ◇ Pony bead
- ◇ Fabric glue
- ◇ Needle tool or heavy-duty toothpick
- ◇ Scissors

Create the spirals. Create six 1 ½" (38mm) spirals, two 1 ¼" (32mm) spirals, four 1" (25mm) spirals, one ½" (13mm) spiral, and four 1" (25mm) teardrops with 1 ½" (38mm) drops. Glue the teardrops together as shown.

Glue the first layer. Using the Layer 1 diagram as a guide, glue the teardrops, 1 ½" (38mm), 1" (25mm), and ½" (13mm) spirals together.

Glue the second layer. Glue the two 1 ¼" (32mm) spirals on top of the first layer according to the Layer 2 diagram.

Create the necklace and closure. Cut a 15" (381mm) strip of T-shirt yarn, fold back each of the ends to form a loop, and glue the loops closed. Glue the strip to the back of the necklace according to the Back View diagram. Complete the necklace by following the Loop Closure technique on page 8.

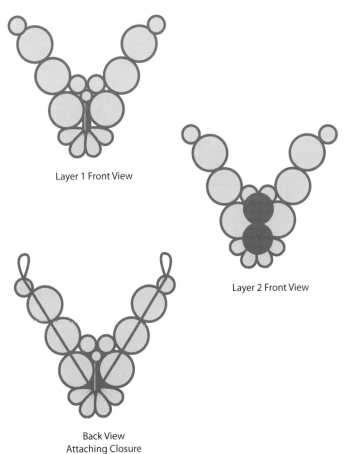

Layer 1 Front View

Layer 2 Front View

Back View
Attaching Closure

Sophisticated Spiral Trio

This set is something special. The projects mix simple and complex designs that come together to form a splendid spiral arrangement.

Necklace

Create the decorative spirals. Create a symmetrical 2" (51mm) S spiral using an 18" (457mm) T-shirt yarn strip (marking the midpoint). Cut eight 9" (229mm) strips, make a mark on each at 6" (152mm), and create eight 1" (25mm) S spirals that are asymmetrical.

Create the necklace spirals. Create two ¾" (19mm) drop spirals with a 16" (406mm) tail, using a 20" (508mm) strip.

Arrange and glue. Place the spirals next to each other in a symmetrical pattern. Carefully add drops of glue at all points where the spirals touch each other. Once the project has dried, create a Bead Pull-Through closure to complete the necklace (see page 7).

SUPPLIES

- Hand-dyed T-shirt yarn
- Earring stud backs
- Pony beads
- Fabric glue
- Fabric marker
- Needle tool or heavy-duty toothpick
- Scissors

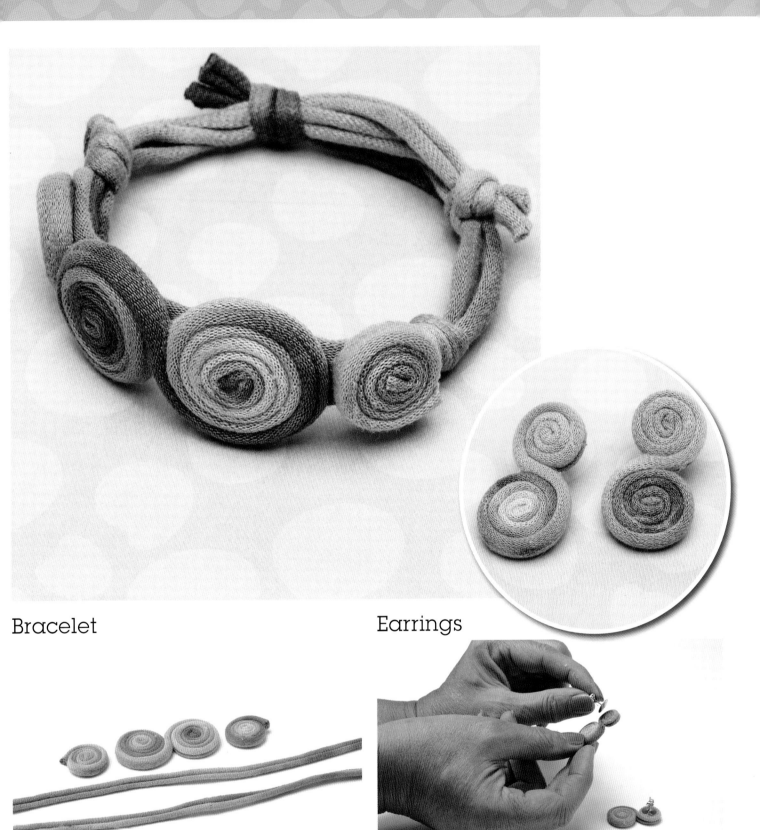

Bracelet

Cut two 16" (406mm) T-shirt yarn strips. Create a symmetrical 2" (51mm) S spiral using an 18" (457mm) T-shirt yarn strip (marking the midpoint), and create two 1½" (38mm) spirals. Lay the two 16" (406mm) yarn strips next to each other, touching, on a flat surface. Glue the S spiral on top of the 16" (406mm) strips, centered along their length. Glue the smaller spirals to each side of the S spiral. Create a Double Knotted Adjustable Closure to complete the bracelet (see page 7).

Earrings

Create a symmetrical 1" (25mm) S spiral using a 9" (229mm) T-shirt yarn strip (marking the midpoint). Alternatively, create asymmetrical spirals by marking at 3" (76mm). Glue earring studs to the back of each of the spirals.

Tonal Teardrop Necklace

This necklace has a delicate floral design that lays beautifully. Mixing several kinds of spirals, the necklace takes a little more time, but is well worth the effort.

SUPPLIES

- ◇ Hand-dyed T-shirt yarn
- ◇ Pony bead
- ◇ Fabric glue
- ◇ Needle tool or heavy-duty toothpick
- ◇ Scissors

1

Create the spirals. Create five 1" (25mm) teardrops, two 1 ¼" (32mm) spirals, and two ½" (13mm) drop spirals with 2" (51mm) drops.

2

Glue the spirals. Glue the five teardrops together along their sides near their points to form a semicircle. Glue one of the large spirals on top of them, over the points of the teardrops.

3

Add the drop spirals. Glue the loose ends of the drop spirals to the large spiral, right above the center teardrop. This is the back of the necklace.

4

Add the tie. Cut a 24" (610mm) length of yarn to be used as the necklace tie and mark the center point. Glue the center segment of the tie all along the top edge of the teardrops, against the large spiral, on the back of the necklace decoration.

5

Finish the necklace. Glue the second 1 ¼" (32mm) spiral on the back of the necklace, over top of the tie and the tips of the teardrops. (Pictured is the back of the necklace.) Create a Bead Pull-Through closure to complete the project (see page 7).

Layer 1 Back View

Layer 1 Back View with Necklace

Layer 2 Back View

Layer 3 Front View